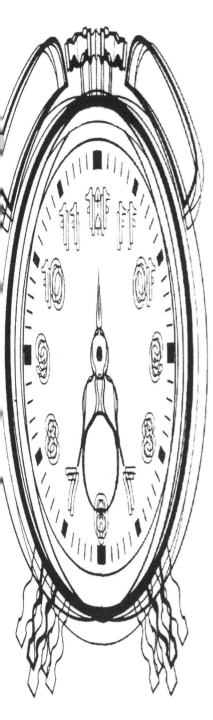

th
two-way
clock

poems

Sydney
Carter

© 1969, 1971, 1974, 2000 Sydney Carter

The Two-Way Clock first published in 1974 included
the following collections of poetry:

Nothing Fixed or Final first published in 1969.
Love More or Less first published in 1971.
The Feel of Wood first published in 1974.

Reprinted in 2000, including the poem *Love too late.*

Published by Stainer & Bell Limited,
PO Box 110, Victoria House, 23 Gruneisen Road,
London N3 1DZ, England.

ISBN 0 85249 287 1

CONTENTS

RUN THE FILM BACKWARDS

When I was eighty-seven
they took me from my coffin:
they found a flannel nightshirt
for me to travel off in.

All innocent and toothless
I used to lie in bed,
still trailing clouds of glory
from the time when I was dead.

The cruel age of sixty-five
put paid to my enjoyment:
I had to wear a bowler hat
and go to my employment.

But at the age of sixty
I found I had a wife,
And that explains the children.
(I'd wondered all my life.)

I kept on growing younger
and randier and stronger
till at the age of twenty-one
I had a wife no longer.

With mini-skirted milkmaids
I frolicked in the clover:
the cuckoo kept on calling me
until my teens were over.

Then algebra and cricket
and sausages a-cooking,
and puffing at a cigarette
when teacher wasn't looking.

The trees are getting taller,
the streets are getting wider.
My mother is the world to me:
and soon I'll be inside her.

And now, it is so early,
There's nothing I can see.
Before the world, or after?
Wherever can I

be?

THE SIN OF BEING

What trouble maker
sent us all
into this giddy,
death-defying Fall

out of the dark
into the light?
Who dared to break
the peace of night?

Oblivion
keeps pulling me
toward the paradise
of not to be

but still I
disobey the call:
the sin of being is
Original.

CHILD

I am your laughing, crying,
possibility:
I keep on coming as
I did before,

hoping and hungering
and with no visible
means of support
whatever.

Naked need is
all I offer:
my extremity is
your opportunity,

my Bethlehem
is where you can be born.
And you will be
King Herod to yourself?

Look in the mirror of
my cradle, see
your laughing, crying,
possibility,

hoping and hungering
and with no visible
means of support
whatever.

MY DANCING DOUBT

The prizes and medals which I find,
turning the cupboard out, now seem to have
nothing to do with me.

I can account for all the scars of shame
and horror that I carry; not for my
hope and hilarity.

I wore the mask that nature handed out
of being English, old or young, a male,
married or otherwise.

Where was I really living all the while?
I played the conscientious hypocrite
and persecuted doubt

Which flowered like a faith turned inside out,
dancing and lyrical, and made a mock
of all my history,

Laughing at solemn Boy Scout promises,
badges and wedding rings by which I tried
but vainly to commit

What cannot be committed. For the tail
can never wag the dog. My centre is
not where I thought it was.

THE HOLY MOUNTAIN

Excepting in
the Saturnalia
the slave is not the master.

There is no
equality between
the rich and poor, the

Ugly and beautiful,
the young and old,
the living and the dead.

The lion will not
lie down with the lamb
in Africa.

So each must learn
to keep his proper place.
What that may be

Is problematical,
for this does not
rule out a revolution.

Even so, you're
either up or down,
you cannot be

both male and female,
black and yellow or
stupid and brilliant

excepting in
that Holy Mountain which
is only found

Upon the map of love.

BY THIS SEA

By this sea
the time is always early,
here there is
no end and no beginning.

While you are growing up
and marrying
and growing down again
and looking at

the clock and the calendar,
beside this sea
the time is always early,
here there is

no clock or calendar,
your life and death
are dancing with each other,
here there is

no end and no beginning,
by this sea
the time is always early.

SHOULDER

My wailing shoulder
woke me in the night.
I want a hot water bottle.
Go to sleep.
I want the feel of fingers.
Go to sleep.
*Show me you love me or I'll
haunt you like
a banshee till the morning.*
I got up
and made a cup of tea
and waggled my
left arm about a little.
Blood and bone
obey my wishes in the
daylight, but they
make me listen to them
in the night.

CHRIST'S HOSPITAL

Tea bell is calling and the London train
Is fading homeward. I am left alone.
My bands are crooked and a coward wind
Is blowing through my bone.

The bullies in The Magnet and The Gem
Were all substantial, but I face a lout
Without a body: being homesick was
A thing Bob Cherry never knew about.

You haloed heroes of the world of School,
Tom Brown, Tom Merry, intercede for me!
Make me glad that I'm a Bluecoat Boy
And dull this ache I feel for Battersea.

My buckle is silver now. The blubbing past
Is buried underneath a football field.
Nothing will ever be so bad again.
The well is empty and the wound is healed.

Butter is turned to flab and tea to kiff
And home is here and not in Battersea.
A ghost is whining in the Cockney night
Where flab is butter still, and kiff is tea.

My bell's a bugle now, my buckle brass.
I go to school again but cry no more.
The siren weeps for all the world tonight
And I am not alone now, as before.

Come back into my body, Cockney ghost
Of all I used to be and cannot kill:
The past is never over, till I'm dead
I fight the bully of my boyhood still.

IN CORAM FIELDS

Adam is
naming the animals,
and Eve is just

about to eat an apple,
Icarus
is flying for a fall,

Prometheus
is playing with the matches,
up the wall

Columbus climbs,
looks over: no Japan,
only America.

In Coram Fields
the world is being tasted,
tested for

the first time is
for ever.

ST. ANDREW'S (DISUSED) BURIAL GROUND

Along the Gray's Inn Road
The 18 buses rumble.
Like Easter Island statues
We sit here and we crumble.

Will next year's summer find us
Above the sod or under?
And who will win the 3 o'clock?
That is what we wonder.

The dusty wind is blowing,
The dead leaves dance a ballet.
The children read the tombstones,
But we prefer *Reveille*.

Here comes that croaking keeper
To tell us that it's late.
Go home, and fill your pools in.
I want to shut the gate.

Go home and fill your pools in,
You've got a chance of winning.
Until the world is over
You're still at the beginning.

BRITISH MUSEUM

Round the groove I go
playing my boyhood back:
the disc is called
the British Museum.

Every stone is still
electric with the past.
My hope and lust
keep bouncing back at me.

A letter from
John Keats to Fanny Brawne,
a Roman bust,
a Buddha made of wood,

the naked girls
still dancing for dead Pharaoh,
this great fist
of granite, punching out

(recalling, though
I can't remember why
my Confirmation and
religious doubt)

welcome me to the club
of those who die:
King Pharaoh and
the dancing girls and I

now know each other better.
Full of guilt
and fear of the consequence
I used to be.

Now I am older
I am not so shy;
I'll bite the apple deep,
before I die.

LOVE FROM MANCHESTER

You were my friend
before you married me.
But now I am too close
for you to see.

Together, we're alone.
From far away
you write in letters what
you never say.

By separation
you are blind no more.
From Manchester you love me
as before.

STATUE

On the auction
block I stand,
exiled from
my native land.

Doctor-like
the dealers come,
prod my belly
with a thumb,

Clinically
estimate
authenticity
and date

Expertise
in beauty must
be impersonal
like lust

And ignore
the sentimental,
catalytic,
incidental,

Dead and buried
private part
in a public
work of art.

Root and tendril
in the past
perish like
the flesh at last,

But my beauty
travels on
tougher than
a skeleton.

ONE TRACK

I am the goddess with the one track mind
love means one thing and one alone to me
my purpose procreation
boy or girl
cheesemite or mackerel the more you mate
and multiply the better
in or out
of lawful wedlock for morality
is not what I am here for
happiness
is not what I am here for
love or hate
each other but (for god's sake)
copulate.

RIDDLE

Pale in the dark
before the break of day
I turn a dusky pink
or golden yellow
just as the sun is rising.

Passing through
brown in the morning
I may ripen to
jet black at noon
or even midnight blue.

The dying day
shrivels my colour to
a kind of grey,
and in the night
there's nothing left of me
but what is white.

NO GENTLEMAN

My lord,
ten thousand pounds for breach of promise is
more than I can afford;
so let me say
before this court and all the world today
that though I'd rather see this lady dead
I'm asking her to marry me instead.

A HUNDRED YEARS AGO

A hundred years ago
is coming closer now,
it used to be
the Battle of Waterloo
but now it is the
Charge of the Light Brigade.

At last I see
how things creep up on you
and here and now
turn into history.
A hundred years
is just my lifetime
multiplied by two.

But I am still the child
they woke one night
to see a Zeppelin
when Kaiser Bill
was still a bogey man
and Kitchener
more famous than his valet.

Do not be
fooled by the clock;
though Cleopatra is
no longer visible,
all history
is just a here and now
you cannot see.

YOUR DANCING BODIES

Your dancing bodies
show to me
the shape of what
must surely be
though when and where
I cannot see.

I pluck the promise
from the thorn:
until I die
it will be worn.
For this alone
I have been born.

Though when and how
is hard to guess
the promise will be kept:
for less
I cannot settle
or say yes.

THE FUTURE IN THE PAST

In that past
the future lives for ever,
what I hope
is still around the corner.

Sailing from
Piraeus in the sunlight
I could see
the lighthouse, far ahead.

I registered
that later we would pass it.
Now and then
I took a look at it:

the lighthouse never
came any closer.
We took photographs
and danced upon the deck.

At six o'clock
the sun began to set,
the tawny hills, suddenly,
turned to lilac.

Then I saw
the future in the past:
the lighthouse was
behind me on the left.

14

But when I smell
lime trees in flower
I am seventeen,
and walking in Geneva.

In that past
the future lives for ever,
what I hope
is still around the corner.

NO WAY BACK

Lean on the future. There
if anywhere
you walk upon the water.

All that was true at first
is true at last
but there is no way back
into the past

But through the future. There
if anywhere
the miracle must happen.

ROMANTIC LANDSCAPE

Lifting and carolling from tip to tip
of the uplifted water, drowning light
is playing ducks and drakes.

The rising wind
keeps an appointment with the waiting wood.
A million dark green girls are passionate,
weeping, anonymous.

A tethered boat
tugs in a wild, reflected agony
of adolescent longing, with one eye
fixed on the looking glass.

THE MIRACLE

Tight as a headache
the congested crags
hem in the traveller

but suddenly
the humped obsession cracks
and clapping waves
cry alleluia.

With my fingers cupped
I kneel again
by the forgotten lake,
lifting infinity.

MY WICKED CORNS

Come, beauty,
sweep me off my feet:
I long to levitate,
the wicked corns
of self are killing me.

ROBINSON CRUSOE

Robinson Crusoe
had no bottom he could
kick, when he felt like it,
except his own.
Hell may be other people:
that is what
Robinson needed and,
at last, he got.

16

THIS BLACK LIGHT

Resurrection is
remembering,
being remembered by
the other end of
all I ever am.

And though my flesh
upon the cross of time
may feel forsaken,
even flesh can look
(without the help of

any priest or book)
toward the resurrection
of the dead and
life in a world to come.
Blind loving is a

kind of believing
and remembering and
being remembered by
the other end
of all I ever am

and led by this
dumb gospel of the body,
this black light,
all creatures learn to travel
through the night.

34 TO 17

You who are 17
blame me because
the world is in a mess.

When I was seventeen
we talked about
the Treaty of Versailles

And so we pass
the buck right back to Adam;
so let me

Ask, in the name of
my small son,
aged 3,

About insecticide,
the colour bar,
the H bomb
and the pill.

You will be 31
when he is 17.
What (if anything)

Will you have done
to dodge the accusation
of my son?

THE PRESENT TENSE

Your holy hearsay
is not evidence:
give me the good news
in the present tense.

What happened
nineteen hundred years ago
may not have happened:
how am I to know?

The living truth
is what I long to see:
I cannot lean upon
what used to be.

So shut the Bible up
and show me how
the Christ you talk about
is living now.

ALMANACK

JANUARY
    Look forward
or look backward
I am both
the end and the beginning.

FEBRUARY
    This is the weary
Tuesday of the year:
too late and yet
too early.

MARCH
    Spring has become
a possibility:
the hares
are going mad.

APRIL
    The sepulchre
cracks open.
Jesus Christ! Or
is it a daffodil?

MAY
    This is the lucky and
unlucky month:
all things are
adolescent.

JUNE
    This is the time you
long for, and you fear.
This is the summer and
the Test is here.

JULY	It's now or never. Though the grass is wet don't wait for weather you may never get.
AUGUST	Lift up a shell and you will hear the sea, your mother, whispering "Come back to me"
SEPTEMBER	A sudden twinge of frost: but see, the sun! It was a false alarm.
OCTOBER	Halloween: and this is where you face the facts of death.
NOVEMBER	The Sun is bleeding on a field of fog. Remember two World Wars.
DECEMBER	Look for the sunlight in your wood and stone, look for the skygod in your blood and bone.

OCTOBER

How many more of these
surprisingly sunny days
before the year is over?

The Spring was promising,
The Summer was
a disappointment.

20

Now the ruined year
went faster and faster
till it was too late

to hope for anything.
But suddenly
the clock was paralysed,

the leaves came down
ever so slowly, like the
killing knife in a

Japanese movie.
It was lucky that
the sun was shining

when eternity
made this take-over bid.
But can the year,

dreaming or drowning,
murder time and make
October last for ever?

THE GOOD BOY

Show me the book of rules
the good boy said
I'll be obedient.

The rules of God
are in this Holy Book
the parson said.

But how can I
be sure that
you are right?

You can't be sure.

I have created you
in my own image.
Do you think that I

Crave for security?
Go out upon
a limb, the way I do:

Create a world,
be crucified,
and be obedient

Only to what you are.

Get thee behind me
Satan, the good boy said
I only want

To see the book of rules
the good boy said
to be obedient.

THIS CHOOSING

This choosing is
the cross you have to carry:
right or wrong,
you drag your feet in this
or dance along.

You are not
innocent like the rose
or alligator,
you are condemned to be
your own creator.

Self pity will
not make it any better:
right or wrong
you drag your feet in this
or dance along.

SPORTING CHANCE

God took a chance
when he put Adam and
Eve where the apple was.
Unless the game
was rigged from the beginning
then the Fall
suggests that Luck
not God
is Lord of all.

DOUBT IS

Doubt is what you
drown in or walk upon
the solid deck
is never really solid

singing a carol round
the Christmas tree
you can forget that you
are floating but

the ship is not rock-bottomed
all the while
you walk upon the water
I will love

this dark and
downward pulling
angel doubt
that I could never learn

to dance without

THE FAITH CAME FIRST

The faith came first.
In the beginning was
the way that I believe
and after that
came all that I believe in

Hitler, Christ,
Apollo, Aphrodite
and Karl Marx
fruit, thorn or
flower on
a single tree.
Faith is the sap of it.

By faith I test
the gospel of St. Matthew,
Michelangelo,
Bach or the Beatles
but
the faith came first, I see
no other rock
but this to
build upon.

THE BREAD

This is the bread: the most important thing
to do with it, is eat it.

Who baked the loaf and how, who sowed the seed
is relevant. But all of that can wait.

And how the universe, of which this loaf
is a fantastic part, first came to be

Is worth a thought; which you will never have
unless you learn to eat.

How anything can ever be at all is
something to wonder at; for none can live

By bread alone, but show me any who
can get along without it. This is where

All faith and wonder start: by eating and
by drinking what is offered. This is the

Body and Blood: the sacrament you take
or commit suicide.

BOX OF MATCHES

My box of matches
can amaze the night:
the darkness cannot
comprehend the light.

Blackness, oblivion
and death require
no explanation:
but this stab of fire

Strikes at the root
of probability.
That light, or anything,
could ever be

Is most improbable;
but here I stand
holding a box of matches
in my hand.

And all my faith and all my
logic spring
from the first, sudden and
unlikely thing.

NO COPYRIGHT

This is the song
that has no copyright.
The pagans and the jews
can sing another lyric
if they choose.

The christian publishers
cannot agree;
they think this music
is their property.

They still expect
a moral ten per cent
they can't collect.

THE QUESTION AND THE ANSWER

Upon this cross
you must be crucified
for I am both

The question and the answer.
To create
is to be crucified,

The son must learn
to fashion like the father.
In the hour

When I forsake you
you will find that you
are now the question

And the answer too.

THE DANGER

I am the danger that you crucify.
Bury or burn me, but I will not die.

I am the danger you are sure to meet
When walking to Emmaeus; and though sweet

The name of Jesus Christ may be to you
I am both Jesus and not Jesus, too.

I am the danger coming from the East
Now tame and welcome at your Christian feast:

I am the danger coming from the West,
I am the wild and unexpected guest.

I am the life inside you: lean on me
and say goodbye to your security

And do not look for safety in the sky.
Can you be braver (do you think) than I?

FASHION SHOW

Impudent beauty
of a girl named Mouche
stepping along the catwalk

preaches a sermon
to remind me that
guilt is unnecessary,

there is another way
to be alive, but
I had forgotten it.

Sin is forgiven
and the gift of grace is
still to be found

in unexpected places.

MY FLAT-EARTH LOGIC

My flat-earth logic will not
get me anywhere,
for east turns into west
and even what
I prove impossible
I know is not.

To reason that is round
effect and cause
give birth to one another:
last and first
explode for ever in
a single burst.

End and beginning
in a circle go.
I built my house in time,
in spite of that,
as if the globe I'm on
were really flat.

CAROLE

Lifting and loving you
that I am not
and yet your body is
my bone and blood
I wonder at the maker
who can be
before I was and yet
come after me.

Round in the everlasting
carole go
my end and my beginning:
I can see
the circle I am part of.
Son and mother,
father and daughter follow
one another.

Now is the time and place
of Bethlehem:
wearing my body now
you caper high
for each and all of us.
I laugh to see
my own life leaping in
and out of me.

THE CANDLELIGHT

I am the candlelight.
I do not say there is a god,
I only say hullo.

Out of the nothingness
I most improbably come
and back again I go.

I am no messenger.
The thing I actually am
is all I ever show.

By me you travel up the stairs
to bed,
By me you read the gospel
of St John.

My fire is physical.
I have a body made of wax
and soon it will be gone.

I am a miracle like
you, I contradict the night
and then I travel on.

TRAVELLING THE BALLAD

Love is in the ballad.
I travel through
a bad part of the ballad,
yet I trust
the love that is in the ballad,
for I must.

Panic is in the ballad.
I ride upon
my nightmare in the ballad:
courage gone,
I cling by fingertips but
travel on.

My flesh is in the ballad.
I travel on
a body through the ballad.
He or she,
I ride the other who
is riding me.

Despair is in the ballad,
I travel through
a desert in the ballad.
I can see
no sign of water, not
a single tree.

My death is in the ballad.
I travel to
the last part of the ballad.
Lose or win,
though I go down with it,
my trust is in

The love that is in the ballad.
Though I am
forsaken in the ballad,
yet I trust
the love that is in the ballad,
for I must.

ADVICE

Do what
You're told
and
Be yourself
they said
Think young
Grow up
Look lively
and
Drop dead
You too
Can be a
Teenage
Centenarian
an Honest
Butcher
and a
Vegetarian.

IN THE BLACK ENAMEL

You were like Christmas,
always coming: then, suddenly,
you were there. In khaki with
a kit bag full of badges.

A volunteer, you
rose to lance-corporal. Your chest was bad,
they sent you to a convalescent home,
you never got to Flanders. But you had
a lean and military step, also
an ebony walking stick, a present to
you from your officer. You twirled it as
you went up Highgate Hill.

You had a cupid's mouth with a red moustache,
and in a box I found a silk top hat.
Before the War
you must have been a masher. Mother
hinted at goings on; but you had also
taught in a Sunday School.

Waltzing around the room, you'd sing about
the Romany Rye and sometimes you would
take down The Poets: read us Tennyson
or Ella Wheeler Wilcox or (my favourite)
a bit of Hiawatha. Shakespeare was
in rather tiny print but he was there
with Dickens, on the shelf. You bought,
but never played on, a piano.
Your weekly Books were
Tit-Bits, Answers, The News of the World and
The Amateur Gardener. You liked to wear
a rose in your lapel. Your paper was
The Westminster Gazette.

Your voice was Cockney with a kind of
posh grandiloquence. You voted Tory,
were not ashamed of being working class but
longed for nobility. You told me that
our ancestors were French, aristocratic
(before the Revolution) but at another time
you told me they were Jewish. Balancing the
hope against the probability
you never could be sure. But either way
the legend could be true. Over or
under the Rembrandt rabbi, you could see
the Laughing Cavalier.

Your laughter is
what I must not forget:
Romany Ryeful and sky-blooded, I
can hear it lifting still,
forgiving me
like God for what I hoarded. Love is what
you needed most, I see; and now, though late, I
bring you a bucketful.

Bare-chested in
the Brompton Hospital and flat against
the cold X ray machine, you startle me:
I see you, eye to eye and bone to bone
there in the black enamel.

5TH OF NOVEMBER

Locked in the Little Ease,
your long bones bent,
your manhood cracked, your marrow
leaking out,
my fellow mask,
what do you think about?

Do you cry out that
Christ has promised us
not peace, but gunpowder,
and claim the cup
of him who came
to blow the whole world up?

You are no gentle Jesus,
but a Fox,
a farmyard Judas
that we have to kill:
So we can rack you
With a righteous will.

A London crucifixion
lies ahead:
the rope, the hurdle and
the butcher's block.
But like a looking glass
you burn and mock

All men who mock you, saying
"None is safe
in such a world as this and
in November
I call you by the bonfire
to remember:

Until my twisted limbs
are straightened out,
my broken courage mended,
God is locked
and cracked in a Little Ease.
Your Christ is mocked

In every mask you mangle.
Come, then, and pray for
God in all of us on
Guy Fawkes Day."

MY ONLY TRUE BELIEVING

Every time I jumped to
Jesus, I came
back like a boomerang.
My hoping was
my only true believing,
but you said
it could not be like that.

I lived on borrowed faith
until I saw
no way to liquidate
the debt, unless
I turned your economics
inside out:
my only true believing
was my doubt.
You said
it could not be like that.

Can true believing be
conceived, immaculate
of any history?
The future for a father
and the Bible
only a foster father?
No, you said,
it could not be like that.

By love and song I learn
to jump to what
may or may not be there.
I lean at last
on what is in the future,
not the past:
and if you contradict
I quote St Paul:
not faith, but love is
last and first of all.
You shake your head
but do not contradict what I have said.

DOUBTING TOM

The cat is on the mat,
You say. I look.
You tell me it is written
In a book.

Where is that other cat?
I hear no purr,
I see no whiskers and
I feel no fur.

You trust that book
which you are reading from.
But I do not, I am
A Doubting Tom.

WHAT IS IMPOSSIBLE

Shy, awkward, slender
like a daffodil,
you turn in wind and sunlight,
making your
fairy tale promises.

My flesh is listening,
all fairy tales
are picked up by the body.
Making love is
part of the parable.

You wear the mask of Easter,
and I wear
the mask of Halloween.
I shall not take
promises literally.

Safe in the circle of the parable
I'll love and not be mocked.
Never mind
the clock and the calendar.

Scatter your promises
and prophesy
what is impossible,
it does not matter.
There is another I, another you.

What is impossible
could still be true.

IMPERIAL WAR MUSEUM

In this museum of the Skull I
gag upon
the stink of crucifixion.
The gallant drank this cup
with courage, the coward had
to drink it too.
You run away,
they ram it down your gullet.

Gas mask and bayonet are nothing but
the visible tip of this: the rot goes down
right to the gut of God. The tender flesh
is torn and the petal crushed. And who is the
forsaken, the forsaker?

But the lark
still rises up, regardless.
Crazy loves
still crack the rock of logic.
Crucified things
cry Alleluia
and the killer worm
is ransomed by the rose,
the name of God
washed in the blood of Jesus.

REVERSAL

Nailed to my nothingness
I hang forsaken,
How could a loving father
let me doubt?
I face the fact that I
could be mistaken.
How could I be
my father's son without?

By this I prove
his living blood in me,
confound all crosses
and confirm my fate:
Left in the dark, alone,
I learn to be
the brightness that I carry
and create.

HEADLINES

Throats
are cut by
Razors.
You can prove Anything by
Statistics.
Logic,
Sex,
Church Bells,
Theology,
can Drive you Mad.
Clocks should be Abolished.
Times are Bad.

ANGER

I bless this angel that I try to choke
by counting up to ten: this stallion
that will not be castrated, that will die
kicking the stable down.

Touching my cap to Christianity
and singing Gentle Jesus I have called
anger my enemy, I have not faced
the holiness of fire.

Cold in the courtyard where my conscience has
denied ferocity, I listen to
the crowing of the cock. I have not been
true to the mystery.

There is no charity for those who cannot
look at the burning bush, no love that will not
live in the wilderness. I travel back to
look at the burning bush.

HEAL AND SON

Wickedly
I seek the good.
Naked parables
of wood

Preach a sermon
to the soul:
simple things
will make you whole.

Looking at
the price, I see
that for this
economy

I shall pay
more than I should.
Holy shapes
of flesh or wood

dig a pit
to pull you in.
By simplicity,
I sin.

Naked, pure
and Quakerly,
would you make
a rake of me?

MY BELIEVING BONES

Swung by the rhythm of
a yes and no
between the living and
the dead I go.
The dance is in my bones
and though I see
that every dancing bone
will cease to be
I will believe my bones
and learn to trust
my living and my dying,
for I must.

Coming and going by
the dance, I see
that what I am not is
a part of me.
Dancing is all that I
can ever trust,
the dance is all I am,
the rest is dust.
I will believe my bones
and live by what
will go on dancing when
my bones are not.

ANONYMOUS

Forget my name is Jesus.
From now on
I am anonymous.

Do not trust the people who
hang me like a millstone
round your neck.

Do not look at me but
what I am pointing to.
The Jesus who

keeps saying "I am Jesus,
look at me,
there is no substitute"

is an imposter. Do not trust
the Christian cult of
personality, I came

to turn you on and not
to turn you off,
to make you free and not

to tie you up.
*My yoke was easy and
my burden light*

until they made
salvation copyright, and
all in the name of Jesus.

So forget
my name was ever Jesus.
From now on

I am anonymous.

SHAKE YOUR WINGS

Shake your wings
and crow, my liberty!
They put me into prison,
turn the key,
my feathers are bedraggled.
They turn the light off
and I cannot see,
but shake, my life
and show, my liberty!
They break me and
they put me in a coffin.

My life, my love, my
dancing liberty,
where are you now?
They tell me you are dead.
I'm dancing where
I always did, you said.
I have gone down
deeper than the dark is,
I have gone
down and come up again.

I am earlier
than anything whatever.
Shake your wings
and do not look bedraggled.
Liberty is
deeper than your death is,
liberty is
deeper than the dark
can ever be:
so shake your wings
and
show your liberty.

THE BURDEN

A cupid brought up in a monastery
wanted to be approved of.
They clipped his wings and shaved his curls and
with erotic mouth compressed
into a thin straight line, his roving eyes
directed to the ground,
he sternly forbade himself and won the good
opinion of the abbot.

But where did approval get him? This is what he
started to ask himself.
Over the monastery wall he heard two lovers,
on a haystack,
laughing and moaning in a way that made his
feathers itch to flutter.
This he confessed to his superiors, who
gave him penances.
But kneeling before the Crucifix,
he said:
Why do you never laugh? And what about those
lovers on the haystack?

One morning, raking up the autumn leaves, he
started to pirouette.
For this he was gently reprimanded by
those in authority.
Kneeling before the Crucifix, he wondered:
Are you God, anyway?
To his astonishment the wooden Christ
appeared to give a wink.
Was this a miracle, or was it a delusion of the Devil?

Most of the miracles he read about seemed
highly improbable.
Do I believe all this (he asked himself)
and if I do, then why?
He came to the conclusion that it might be true
or (then again) it might not.
If 50 million monks had all been wrong,
God had a sense of humour.
What do you say to that? he asked the Crucifix.
The glassy sweat
was glistening in the sunlight,
the red, coagulated drops of blood
looked grimly realistic.
Quite disconnected from this agony
he heard a skylark singing.

You're not your usual sunny self today
(the abbot said to him,
floating benignly through the cloister on
a cloud of contemplation).
Suddenly he
wanted to kick the abbot.
That is wicked
(he told himself). I should feel guilty but
(he suddenly realised)
I have never felt guilty, all my life, about
anything whatever.

I must be damned (he said one morning as
he rang the bell for mattins).
I have no sense of sin, I only have
a sense of being blamed. I want to love,
to be loved, to belong. And as for God,
he made me what I am.
If I am bad, he should have made me better.
Either these good old monks are all deceived
or I am morally insane (he said)
or maybe God, like Jesus.
In which case
I'd better keep it quiet or
they'll lock me up. But suddenly
his plucked divinity began to prick
the burden of
his levity descended. I can fly!
he shouted to the monks.
The abbot crossed himself and shook his head.
We'll keep on praying for you, son,
he said.

THE IDOL

Bow to the idol in the east;
Believe and you can join the feast.

Unbelief will keep you out;
None can celebrate who doubt.

If you cannot pass the test,
Turn your back and travel west,

Round the world until you find
The living Now they hid behind

The dying Then which blocked the east
And would not let you join the feast.

STILL

Herod and
Judas Iscariot
still
criss and cross
the cradle they were born in.
Peter still
denies himself
and Pilate breaks
the mirror that he looks at.
On the hill
the soldiers nail themselves
to crosses still.

WRITING OUT

The gliding nib
can dance across the paper
capering
to every new beginning,
leaning back
to dot an "i"
or underline and still
keep travelling to
music.

Penmanship
like cooking and architecture
has to be a
Martha to be a Mary,
worship by

fetching and carrying.
The letters must be
recognisable,
the spelling right,

the punctuation proper.
Laborare
has to be *orare.*
Clarity can
plod,
or levitate like charity.

SOMETHING IS HAPPENING

Dead or not
the star is signalling,
at Jodrell Bank
the needle is still jumping.
Here and now
it happened yesterday
and then and there
it will arrive tomorrow.

Tambourine,
bell, steeple,
stained glass window,
Torquemada
Moody and Sankey
and the rector who
was killed in
a lion's cage

Are shaken by
refracted messages.
In other time
something is happening,
the stone is dropped,
the waves are rippling
and here and now
the news is still arriving.

THE HOLY BOX

The Bible had been rolled away,
The Holy Name of Jesus lay

Like crumpled linen on the floor.
A stranger stood beside the door.

"You will not find him here," he said.
"This is the dwelling of the dead.

You put him in a holy box
But he has shattered all the locks.

By Christ or any other name
The shape of truth would be the same."

I woke, and it was eight o'clock.
I heard the crowing of a cock,

I heard the tolling of a bell.
The church was standing: all was well,

I knew the Bible, thick and black,
Was safe upon the eagle's back.

How could Jesus be the same
If he had another name?

Holy, holy is the box.
Nobody can break the locks.

SPARK ME OFF

Ring telephone
Crack wafer
Kitchen clock
Chip off the seconds on
Your chopping block
Break, water on the shingle

Stink gunpowder
Prick pepper
Bonfire smoke
Reek and rake my life up
Onions poke
And jerk me like a weepy

Spurt, Swan Vesta
Dazzle mirror
Flash
Wilkinson razor blade
Cascade the cash
Glitter it on the counter

Crow, cock of all creation
Crack the crib
Of nothingness and tickle me
A rib
Explode the one and make
A sparking two
I cannot be itself
Without a You.

WHAT EVERY BODY KNOWS

What every body knows
is suddenly
self contradictory,

By love I learn
to dance upon my grave,
to laugh at my

Mortal arithemetic
that cannot see
that one and one

Make more or less than two.
By love I see
the deathless, dancing one

Of you and me.
By love I levitate,
and yet

By inborn gravitiy
I soon forget.
I'll build a tabernacle

On this spot
to make me wise again
when I am not.

LOOK AT THE MOON

Look at the moon,
now you can walk upon it.
Look at granite,
you can chop it up,
walk on it,
worship in it, All
solidity
is still a mystery.

Though landed on,
the moon is a Mona Lisa.
Women are
much closer than the moon
yet still I cannot
tell what is happening.
The Rorschach Test
is all you ever get.

You travel with
the question that you carry,
query keeps on
spinning like a spider,
acrobatically
swinging upon
itself and distance grows
or withers with the looker,

This moon rock will
keep receding for
the microscope is
really a telescope.
Look at the moon.
It keeps on travelling
and near or far
you never catch it up.

SAMARITAN, BE GOOD TO ME

This bearded Jesus
flapping on the wall
faces a girl
with nothing on at all.

The bombers have come back,
the guns begin.
The holy picture
shivers on a pin.

Locked with my terror
for another night
I look at the halo
and the swinging light.

Still knocking on that
same old Sunday gate.
I shout but we
cannot communicate,

My wounded courage
cannot get relief,
I do not have
the ticket of belief.

This helper is
no help to me at all.
I turn to the icon
on the other wall.

The only faith it calls for
is desire,
The flesh is kinder to me
under fire.

No good Samaritan
has come to me
tonight, except
the body of a She.

RIDDLE

Spoon
to stir a pot with
Stick
to poke a pig with
prick
to procreate with:
cradles rock,
monks meditate on
entertainers shock
churches are split
by me
and nuclear devices
are invented.
On a wave
I ride, I beat a drum,
I stand in stone,
I live and die
on paper.

SPIDERLIKE

Spiderlike
the questions spin
pulling answers
from within.

Spiderlike
they swing about
on themselves turned
inside out.

Though to do it
there must be
something solid,
Like a tree,

Which is not
a part of you
to attach
the answer to,

Yet, (I spin again)
That tree,
is it really
part of me?

What is out
and what is in?
Spiderlike
the questions spin

Am I here
or am I there?
Statements sparkle
in the air

Answers to
the question why
hang like sickles
in the sky,

Every one
a question mark
cutting into
what is dark.

Spiderlike
the spinning night
swings upon the
inner light.

CREATION CROWS

Creation crows
and perfect nothingness is
cracked by the cock of light.
I had no fear
of dying all the while
that I was dead.
Now I am living, I
am full of dread.

Creation dazzles
and oblivion
is split to stars and crosses.
I was not
consulted about this
and cannot see
why anything at all
should ever be.

Creation dances.
Equilibrium
is lurching and rocketing,
and I must dance
or fall upon the deck.
The sea of light
has made me sick, and yet
I fear the night.

Creation laughs
at all my gravity,
compelling me to live
by levity.
I am required
to walk upon the water,
to create,
I sink unless I learn to levitate.

Creation rocks
impossibility,
fathers a miracle:
the living now,
later and earlier
than what is never.
The crowing light has split
the dark for ever.

COMMERCIALS

When I have fears that I
may cease to be
I brew myself a cup
of Co-op tea.
"Is God dead?" is
indigestion.
Take Alkaseltzer, it will
kill the question.

NOT YET IN A MUSEUM

Streamlined and shapely like the killer shark
they worship with their teeth.
I see them through the plate glass window in
the zoo of history.

55

Their institutions are as functional as
a hydrogen bomb.
They shape their time with courage, shoot it
without
pity at a target.

They are my enemies; but safe behind
the crystal wall of time
I can admire their beauty, I can play
the traitor to myself.

I put on the mask of Them, I dare to make
love to my opposite:
I wear their horns and hide, I let their ghost
go raging through my body.

Here and now there is no truce of God,
no Saturnalia
in Sharpesville or the Congo, in Vietnam or
Czechoslovakia.

Here and now is not yet a museum,
Here and now they mean to murder me.
I will make love to them by opposition
and keep a sharp eye on the enemy.

THE LIGHT AND COLOUR

The sharp and comfortable clarity
is blurred and broken up;
these spectacles
were never meant for me.

Only the uncorrected colours are
the way they were before.
I'll rest my twisted
looking on the water

Or the clouds, I'll
turn my puzzled wonder
to where definition
does not matter. I can trust

the boundaries no longer,
Green and blue,
the light and colour of
the world, are true.

BLIND AND DEAF AND DUMB

Looking at a coal black light
earlier than day or night,
Talked to by the dancing word
which is never seen or heard,

Blind and deaf and dumb you grope
with the fingers of your hope.
Heaven is a thing you clutch,
Hell is what you fear to touch.

Christ and Bible, moon and star,
Have no meaning where you are.
What is faith? It is a word
You have never seen or heard.

Living by that coal black light
Earlier than day or night
through the silent dark you go:
how, or why, you do not know.

LOVE MORE OR LESS

This is total drama,
you are in it.
The title of it is
THE WAY THINGS ARE.

On the stage
there is a hero.
The drama is
not what he said and did, for
what he said
we never know for certain,
what he did
is like all history,
improbable,
but not impossible.
You only get
a secondhand report.
Uncertainty
is part of the total drama,
you might even
call it a character.

Look at the total picture:
not at Jesus
only, but at Judas.
What he does is
part of
THE WAY THINGS ARE
and what he does
we never know for certain.

The parables
and the beatitudes
are lyrical, but only
part of this
astonishing production.
This is not
just an anthology
of Golden Thoughts:
your thoughts are
in it too. Uncertainty
goes winding in and out
of all you see.
You must not throw a brick
if, like a cat, it
looks at the Crucifixion.

There is a double Chorus:
Faith and Doubt.
They tell you what is true
and all the time
they contradict each other.
They have supporters in
the audience
They push their pamphlets at you.
Some of them are
agents provocateurs.
You cannot tell
a goody from a baddy.

You can identify
with anyone: with
Pontius Pilate, if
you feel like that.
There is no gilt-edged
guarantee that you
have done what is expected.
No one is
quite sure what is expected.

Only remember this:
that you are free.
What happens on the stage
is meant to be
an aid to total freedom,
not a holy
millstone round your neck.
And if you are afraid of liberty, that's
just too bad. For you
are in it, now,
for better or for worse.

Let it all come at you.
Uncertainty
will not deny you this:
you live, and die.
These are the only
solid facts you get:
the rest is up to you.
Let it all come at you:

Inquisitors,
St Francis of Assisi,
Billy Graham and
the Salvation Army.
Also present in the audience,
part of show, are
Hare Krishna, Freud
the Beatles, Marx
and Marilyn Monroe.
The usherettes
will bring you beer or coffee,
LSD or holy bread and wine.

Up on the stage,
non stop, the epic rolls:
but what you see is
never the total drama.
What you are
is where it has to happen.
What you see is
not the first show
and not the only one
but this has lasted
nineteen hundred years.
The shepherds keep on
coming with their gifts.
For that is where
we find we are today,
at Bethlehem.
It's just begun again.
Do you believe it? That
is not the question.
This question is:
what does it do to you?
That is how
you come into the story.

Does it make you
freer, to see that cradle?
Do you wish
the whole thing had never happened?

Well, it has:
The Parable, if not the history,
is now and tomorrow, never
yesterday.
What does it
do to you?

What does it try to make?
Love, more or less.
You take it or you leave it.
You are free,
you cannot be shed of
your liberty.
How would you like to use it?

What you are in is not
a work of art, but
total revelation.
What you do is
part of the revelation.
What is known is
not, until
you know it. What is shown
is not,
until you show it.

INTERVIEW

Where have you been all the day?
            Fishing with question marks.
            The fish I caught
            are piled up in the basket.
            What I seek
            is deeper than the water.
Where have you been all night?
            Travelling past the flesh,
            beyond the bone,
            until I came to nothing.
            Back again
            I travel in the morning.

So what do you believe in?
                    Nothing fixed or final,
                    all the while I
                    travel a miracle. I doubt,
                    and yet
                    I walk upon the water.
That is impossible.
                    I know it is.
                    Improbability
                    is all you can expect. The
                    natural
                    is supernatural.
Where are you going next?
                    Like you, I ask that question.
                    I can only
                    travel with the music.
                    I am full
                    of curiosity.

THE ELEPHANT

Where is the Elephant? The Elephant
is what I came to see. Too late, they said,
the pub has been pulled down.

But in this second-class museum which
they call the Shopping Centre I have found
a small, demoted idol. Can this be

the totem of South London? Can this be
the actual Elephant? I prophesy
against the lying fact, for I can see

an Elephant ten times the size of this,
high on a column in the open air
and floodlit all night long. I see a square

alive with flying fountains, trees and birds
that like to stand on statues. Let there be
peanut and popcorn sellers. Let me walk

across the street again and not be passed
like water through a sewer so that trucks
can rumble overhead. I prophesy

the liberation of the people and
the putting down of traffic. I can hear
the voice of the Elephant: "That Castle which

I carried I detested. I refuse
to bear it any longer!" We are all
one with the Elephant, that Castle broke

the back of all of us. We shout hooray:
Long live the Elephant! Now from the steps
of Spurgeon's Tabernacle, I can see

the Elephant triumphant, with his trunk
lifted for all of us, and trumpeting
our freedom to the sky.

JACOB'S LADDER

I wonder at the immobility
of objects on a table.
Suddenly,
like Jacob I am dreaming.
Up and down
the whirling ladders of
this solid glass
bottle, the bright atomic
angels pass,
all shouting hallelujah.
I have been
on holy ground, like Jacob.
I have seen
the miracle of matter.

THE SHADOW MAKER

You are the shadow maker.
There was no
guilt till you separated
good and bad,
the darkness and the light.
There could not be
a down without an up.
Let there be God,
you said:
a shadow fell.

HALLOWEEN

The burning leaves
have pricked my life awake.
The muffled sun

goes rolling through the fog.
The guy sits in
a mask upon the pavement.

We'll burn him on the bonfire.
After that
we'll climb the hill to Christmas.

On the last day of term
they let you take
whatever book you like.

I'll lug along my
Bible, the Boys' Own Paper
bound and dated

1886 and read about
those midshipmen who never
die, but stay

young and Victorian,
get good advice
from Dr Gordon Stables:

Take a brisk
rub down with a cold damp towel
I can hear him

calling from his coffin.
Through the past
I peer into the future,

with the dead
I walk among the living.
Looking back

I wonder which are which.
October is
the time of their returning.

Through the smoke
of what is over
and what might have been

We walk and hope and keep
our Halloween.

THE SOUTHWOLD LIGHT

Quietly the Southwold Light
Pricks the logic of the night.

From the pebble-crunching sea
Death comes whispering to me:

"What is not will prove the stronger
I came first, and last the longer."

Quietly the Southwold Light
Pricks the logic of the night.

That the wold could ever be
punctures probability.

With the light I come and go,
By that yes I crack a no.

Quietly the Southwold Light
Pricks the logic of the night.

WAITING

This is the stone
of nothing happening
and must I build

a temple out of this?
The tigers pace their cages,
melancholy

monkeys are masturbating.
Can I build
a temple out of this?

The architects
reject the empty mountains
of the moon in

barracks or hospital,
the engineers
stand with their backs

to my Niagara:
the seconds pour
over my ending world

but none of them are
turning a dynamo.
Time wasted is

the thing that I have most of,
waiting is
rich, like Antarctica.

How can I build
a temple out of this?

THE NEW SONG

Be faithful to the new song
thrusting through your
earth like a daffodil.
Be flexible
and travel with the rhythm.

Let your mind
be bent by what is coming:
making is
a way of being made
and giving birth

a way of being born.
You are the child
and father of a carol,
you are not
the only maker present.

How you make
is how you will be made.
Be gentle to
the otherness you carry,
broken by

the truth you cannot tell yet.
Mother and be
mothered by your burden.
Trust, and learn
to travel with the music.

THE LOOSENING OF THE LEAVES

Autumn blows
the sharp and lonely bugle:
Leaves, fall out,
the summer war is over.
Would you like

to wear the green for ever?
You cannot,
the army is disbanded.
Now you must
learn to be separate,

and lean upon
your gravity,
your levity,
and learn to pirouette
into the arms of

what is coming next.
I tremble at
that Last Post and Reveille,
calling all
things to their travelling.

I shiver with the leaves
and yet I love
that sharp and lonely bugle.

NATURE NOTES

Wild cats have crossed
the Scottish border, I
hear on the radio;
the foxes raid
the dustbins in Herne Hill.
Nature is hitting back.
The wind is mad tonight,
it ripples through
the tree tops like a tiger,
whipping at
roses and blackberries.
No gardener, I welcome all
this wildness in a teacup.
Let my tame old elm be
torn by passion,
Let the moon be
tossed like a Flying Dutchman.
Local boys
are part of Nature too: The Mafia
is here, says the pillar box.
In Half Moon Lane
the telephone kiosk
is wrecked again.
A hedgehog lies
squashed flat upon the tarmac.
Two masked men
have walked into my bank.

NO LUCK, TAM LIN

I stood before you naked.
You were a bit surprised but you pretended
not to have noticed it;
put on a kettle, made a cup of tea,
said it was rotten weather.

I stood before you with
my nose chopped off,
my tongue torn out,
my eyeballs on a string.
You felt for a handkerchief;
To dry your tears, perhaps?
To blow your nose.

How shall I come to you
tomorrow night? How can I tell you
what is happening? Soak myself in petrol,
Light a match, burn like a Buddhist monk?

Your friends and mine
talk on the telephone: Poor Margaret,
Jack is so difficult.
No luck, Tam Lin: your Margaret,
Your Janet, won't believe you
She has never
Looked at the Queen of Fairies.

Eight o'clock: another day begins
They smile at one another.

TOM CAT

Tom cat, you have
a heathen heart.
You love to tear
live things apart.

To save you from
this mortal sin
I feed you dead ones
from a tin,

and round your neck
I hang a bell.
But still you have
a heathen smell.

So I shall take you
to the vet.
We'll make a christian
of you, yet.

OTHER FORMS OF LIFE

Sharing the world with me
are kangaroos
and other forms of life.
These would include
the people over thirty.

Fluttering
their creepy photographs
they claim that they
were young like you and me.
And stranger things
than that are possible.

Butterflies
turn into caterpillars:
caterpillars
find that incredible.

MYTHOLOGY

In the beginning God
was all alone
and spoiling for a fight:
and so, He made the Devil.
You be bad
and I'll be good, he said,
and you and I
can wallop one another.

Then God thought
He'd like to have a pet.
He made a Man
and then he made a Woman,
so that they
could breed with one another.

God himself
stayed single all His life.

THE DEVIL IN THE PULPIT

In the beginning was
Authority:
so do what you are told.

Man is a rotten apple:
what he really wants,
is to be wicked.

Why did God
make such a rotten apple?
Do not ask

the Boss to give a reason.
So, be good:
which is impossible.

All you can do
is wish that you were another
and not You.

TILL BIRTH US DO PART

By birth our one
became a two:
you cling to me,
I cling to you.

My hungry
separated I
must feed on otherness
or die.

Your sacrament
of food and drink
I take before
I learn to think.

Though Christians
and Jews would rather
praise you by
the name of Father,

Bodily
theology
still declares
you are a She.

THE OTHER RIB

She keeps on whispering
and promising
and pulling me the way
you used to do, but

Faithful, I go on living.
Habit, hope
and curiosity have
kept me true, but

Death is the other rib I
lost, and she
will get me into bed
at last, like you.

SEA LEGS

Metaphors are only
more or less
statements are relative
and questions beg

the ground they stand upon.
By yes and no
upon the dipping deck
I come and go.

Stumping and staggering
my words are sick
until they find their sea legs.
There's no chance
of standing still when all things
move and dance.

BURIAL

My love, I can safely
and sincerely say,
now that I bury you.

I love you badly
and I could not see
the way to love you better,

Silent now,
no longer passionate,
you bully me,

I bully you no longer.
We should have
buried each other daily,

You and I.
Every morning, all
the world should die.

LIKE LOT'S WIFE

She was a pillar of integrity,
She would not budge an inch.
She held the truth
so tightly to her heart
that it could not
grow up or wander off.

She could not see
that it was born to travel,
was afraid
her treasure might be stolen.
What she loved
had to be fixed and final.

Like Lot's wife
she weathers on the hill top,
looking back
to where she had been happy.
What she held
once, she will hold forever.

What she loved
is beautiful, but dead.

THE NEXT 10 MINUTES

Cut out the next 10 minutes
Of my life,
I know this walk too well
Join up the tape
And make it snappier.

The minutes I have cut
Are piling up
To days and weeks and years.
How many more
Can I afford to lose?

My natural resources
Are dwindling.
A simple field is worth
A fortune now.
This weary climb

Up Holmdene Avenue
May be the last.
I will declare my love
To scarlet letter boxes, traffic lights,
The feel of fur and wood.

Forgive me, world
For all the time I wasted.
Let me sleep
With both my arms around you;
Say goodnight
And hope to say

Good morning.

BIRTHDAY POEM

To what do you
attribute your
levity, Father Wiliam?

To the fact
that I am upside down,
from my own death

I dangle to my birthday.
There is not
much to look back to, son,

And that it why
I keep on looking forward.
My true love

is coming round the corner,
I am only
homesick for tomorrow.

Hope is what
I have for gravity,
my first is last,

My roots are in
the future,
not the past.

HALLEY'S COMET

The miniskirt
is nearly gone.
The randy sun
is rolling on

to lift the curtain
of the night
from other regions
of delight:

the neck, the navel
or the breast.
Long legs are what
I like the best.

Like Halley's comet
They'll be back
(according to
my Almanack)

but I am getting
old and grey.
I may not live
to see the day.

BRICKS AND MORTAR

I'm married to a bungalow
and rue the day I met it.
I gave my heart to Hampton Court
but I could never get it.

I open my *Observer*
and cast illicit looks
at the latest kinky offering
reported by Roy Brooks.

There's a mortuary chapel
not far from Tavistock
with a bathroom in the belfry
and a creaky weathercock.

There's a ruined railway station
on a very windy moor
with a garage labelled LADIES
and roses round the door.

On Lundy there's a lighthouse
in a pretty shocking state
but you couldn't find a better spot
to sit and meditate.

If I were Rockerfeller
I'd like to buy them all
and let my randy fingers
go running up the wall.

My neighbour need not worry
about his wife or daughter,
my wanton mind is more inclined
to rape of bricks and mortar.

If I were Rockerfeller —
but time and cash are fleeting,
I'll try to love my bungalow
and put in central heating.

SHOCK ME, DOCTOR

I am not a normal man.
Cure me, doctor, if you can.
Banish by electric wire
My unnatural desire.

Flash those pictures on a screen,
Therapeutic but obscene;
When it is a naked girl
Wave a flag and ring a bell.

But if it should be a boy
Punish my Platonic joy
Shock me, doctor, through and through
Till I feel the same as you.

Turn my liking to disgust,
Fill me up with proper lust;
Wash my brain until I fit,
Make me think a miss a hit.

THE HOLY HORSES

You ride
the holy horses
your yellow hair is
kinder than
your heart is.
You ride
the holy horses,
your body
cannot lie.

Your body is
a preacher
and your long legs
are truer than
your words are.
You ride
the holy horses.
Your body
cannot lie.

Your shape is
hallelujah.
You show the light,
although
you cannot see it.
You ride
the holy horses.
Your body
cannot lie.

A hunter and
a healer,
you pull me
one way, and then
you pull another.
You ride
the holy horses.
Your body
cannot lie.

IN THE NIGHT

Blake and Michelangelo
told me it was time to go.
Keats and Shelley cut me dead.
Byron would not turn his head.

Satan told me to be good
and go to church the way I should.
Jesus told me to rebel
quickly, or I'd go to hell.

Waking up, I could not see
why such a dream should come to me.
I took my Bible down and read
a chapter and went back to bed.

Matthew, Mark, Luke and John
bless the bed that I lie on.
Frisk and keep it free from sin
Stop hi-jackers getting in.

THE COMFORTERS

For twenty years
you kept on walking through us.
Windows let in
ordinary daylight. It was not
the time for you to see us.

But tonight
something is different,
Your now and then
are not the way they were.
You shiver, as

you listen to the music.
Was it grief
that cracked your looking open?
You are right,
you listen to the dead.

Turn round and
look at us. For twenty years
we waited in the doorway.
Now you see
the way that the world

is haunted.
Twenty years
you kept on walking through us,
but tonight
I think that you will see us.

IN ARNHEM LAND

In Arnhem Land the aborigines
hunted to eat until the white man came.
He brought a new word: WORK

What could it mean? Experience
taught them that to work
meant doing what
the white man told them to.
They tried it,
but they did not like it much.

Hunting was different.
Hunting was something which you had to do,
but hunting was not work.
Hunting was simply being.
Making love,
making a boomerang was being,
and to walk about was being.

There was a pattern,
you could wander round it.
There was a rhythm,
you could travel with it.
But
to work was not like that.

They were a backward race, the White Man said.
They wore no clothes,
they had no word for God.
They had no word
for Work.

MOTHER TERESA

No revolution will come in time
    to alter this man's life
    except the one
    surprise of being loved.

It is too late to talk of Civil Rights,
   neo-Marxism,
   psychiatry
   or any kind of sex.

He has only twelve more hours to live.
   Forget about
   a cure for cancer, smoking, leprosy
   or osteo-arthritis.

Over this dead loss to society
   you pour your precious ointment,
   wash the feet
   that will not walk tomorrow.

Mother Teresa, Mary Magdalene,
   your love is dangerous, your levity
   would contradict
   our local gravity.

But if love cannot do it, then I see
   no future for this dying man or me.
   So blow the world to glory,
   crack the clock. Let love be dangerous.

LOVE TOO LATE

Love too late
love you were looking for
I have found
but here you are no more...
In time and out...
we talk to one another now
saying all the things
we should have said before...

Printed and bound in Great Britain by Caligraving Limited